PRAISE FOR *I TELL HENRIETTA*

Tina Barry's astonishing collection *I Tell Henrietta* explores thresholds between the dream world and wakefulness, and between poetry and prose. Throughout this book, Barry shares truths of girlhood and womanhood, showcasing moments that drift from real into surreal. While the speaker's confidante in the collection is often the figure of Henrietta, the reader also feels like an intimate part of the storytelling, privy to wonders like, "rivers swirled black, trees pulled from their roots, / tipped to the ground." Barry has a talent for recasting ordinary scenes in a way that transforms them into deeply felt revelations that resonate far beyond the page.
—Mary Biddinger, author of *Department of Elegy*

Tina Barry's startling and eclectic *I Tell Henrietta* pushes the hybrid aesthetic envelope forward. Part poetry, part micro, these written gems are vividly unclassifiable. Suffused with astute observation, memory and crystalline imagery, Barry's collection is a must-read for those who love small works containing multitudes.
—Nathan Leslie, editor of *Best Small Fictions*, author of *Hurry Up and Relax*

Line up the poems in Tina Barry's *I Tell Henrietta* on the bar and take them like shots (alluring, astringent) without any chaser. When you wake up, dare the mirror. You'll find wing-scars, a cigarette burn or two, tattoos you can't remember getting, all love's bruises. And you'll thank Barry for every single mark.
—Joshua Davis, author of *Reversal Spells in Blue and Black*

In *I Tell Henrietta*, Tina Barry draws us into a world both familiar and startling. Her stories are filled with absent fathers who are "with the circus," swans in unexpected iterations, and teenagers "narrow as needlefish." Barry's stories are shared with the elusive title character Henrietta, who listens, sometimes skeptically, but who always elicits more. These poems are soft explosions of beautiful imagery and language and heart. A rich and satisfying read, a journey you will be glad you have taken.

—Francine Witte, author of *RADIO WATER*

I TELL HENRIETTA

TINA BARRY
art by KRISTIN FLYNN

I Tell Henrietta
First Edition 2024 © Tina Barry
All rights reserved

Published in the United States of America by
AIM Higher, Inc.
West Hurley, New York

ISBN
979-8-9863699-2-1 (Hardcover)
979-8-9863699-3-8 (Paperback)

Library of Congress Control Number: 2024940544

Book designer: Shanna Compton
Photographer: Jim Smith
Copy editor: Cindy Hochman of "100 Proof" Copyediting Services
Back cover poem: "My Year of Drawing Swans" by Tina Barry

Cover art: *Swan Song*, 14" x 11", acrylic/panel, 2023 © Kristin Flynn

Ordering & Contact
do@aimhigher.org

*To Bob Barry–my favorite surfer,
and to my mother, Rosalind Ehlin—thank you for the lilies.*

CONTENTS

PROLOGUE
13   My Year of Drawing Swans

I MENTION THE DEER
17   Why Chinchilla Is My Favorite Fur
18   Telling Lies
19   Lily World
20   So, Your Father
21   Another Haunting
22   I Mention the Deer
23   Henrietta Wonders What Haunts Me

I TELL HENRIETTA WHY MERMAIDS UPSET ME
27   Why Mermaids Upset Me
28   I Mention Our Neighbors' Luau
29   The Deep End
30   Henrietta Hints at Secrets

THE JITTERING NIGHT
35   My Father's Mistress
36   Ed Sullivan's Fault
37   The Other Place?
38   Before Nanny Cams
39   Visitation

ZEUS, AGAIN

- 43 Outliers
- 44 Life Drawing
- 45 Henrietta Asks about My Sex Life
- 46 What about Joy?
- 47 Oh, the Carnies
- 48 Rock Lobster!
- 49 Zeus, Again

THE UPSIDE OF LOSS

- 53 Questioning the Lake
- 54 Upside of Loss
- 55 Vanessa
- 56 Before I Left My Boyfriend
- 57 Dog Psychic
- 58 And Wonders about Old Lovers
- 59 I Tell Henrietta about Rusty
- 60 Why I Married a Surfer

HER LIFE NOW

- 65 "*Ghosts?*" Henrietta Asks
- 66 While My Mother Dreams of Judge Judy
- 67 Her Life Now
- 68 After,

HENRIETTA QUESTIONS MY FAITH

- 73 Henrietta Questions My Faith
- 74 Arrival
- 75 In the Tattoo Shop,

EPILOGUE

79 The Swan Returns, This Time with a Russian Accent

81 About the Paintings
82 Acknowledgments
84 About the Author
84 About the Artist
85 About the Publisher
86 Colophon

PROLOGUE

MY YEAR OF DRAWING SWANS

When the need to render a beak lived inside me,
I'd swing one arm around a subway pole,
press the lead point of the pencil into the notebook
I carried.

A dark dot launched the curve of hard bill. Between its eyes,
the black knob, gateway to the swoosh of neck.
Stashes of swan studies filled the drawer of my bedside table.

I'd wake to the sky slouching off its cape and label their parts,
a new language I couldn't stop writing: *lore, nares. Covert*:
its ledge of wings; the serrated *lamella* surrounding its tongue.
At jobs I loathed, I'd peek at torn pieces stuffed into folders;
darken a wing, shadow the water.

Once I had perfected the dusty diamond
of its foot, the center digit so real I could feel
its scalloped ridges with my finger,
I stood in the subway, poised to draw,
but the swans never returned to me.

I MENTION THE DEER

WHY CHINCHILLA IS MY FAVORITE FUR

The last dress my mother bought while we still had money was gray wool, tight to the knees, the hips circled in chinchilla. She wore it to a wedding on a ship, a few fancy dinners, and when my father left, it became her date dress. Later, it served as part of a suit for work: worn under a jacket, as if she hid the animal beneath. When the seams frayed, she cut the fur from its dying host, hung it in the back of the closet. I'd sit in the airless dark, the pelt pressed to my face, inhaling its memory of rodent musk, whiff of seawater, and a scent I thought of as loneliness—the animal's or Mother's, I could never tell.

TELLING LIES

After my father left, I told the babysitter that I bit my nails because my mother refused to cut them. I told my mother that the school secretary was retiring and she should apply for the job. The secretary told my mother that at 40 she was nowhere near retirement age. I told my art teacher, Phil Stein, aka "El Steino," that I knew Picasso and that he admired my work. And I told my class that my father wouldn't be attending parent/teacher night because he was training tigers with his circus troupe in Florida.

My teacher peered over her glasses, frowned. She had met my father, an insurance agent who wore suits, not silver tights, and carried a briefcase, not a whip. My teacher called that night. After a few minutes, I heard the phone slam, braced myself for mother's howl. I expected some kind of punishment. Maybe a TV curfew: Lights out after *Bonanza*. Into bed before *The Ed Sullivan Show*. Instead, she asked, "Why are you telling stories about Dad?" I shrugged. I had grown tired of saying, "He's away on business."

LILY WORLD

Two hours from suburbia to heaven. Gasoline stinks the bus terminal. Cabbies swerve, flip each other off, horns' painful music. Mother's cheeks pinken. The museum's revolving door whooshes us into marble and glass. Crowds of women in wide wool skirts, scarlet lipstick, cashmere.

And then . . . Monet's lilies, ponds of water lilies, whole conventions of lilies. Frills of lavender, shimmering sage, and so many blues; more blues than an ocean or a sky. Pistils exhaling, petals unfurling, a floral striptease. We try for words but can only make sound: "ooo" and "mmm." We don't believe in God. Can't tell you what *spiritual* means. But that hushed room. Those flowers.

SO, YOUR FATHER

A Ferris wheel plays tinkly tunes. Skinny, big-nosed, curly-haired, taller than the three grinning wiseguys he stands with on the beach. He's gobbled two Nathan's hot dogs, savors pepper and sweet onions. At sixteen, he can barely swim. Tries to linger at the shoreline, let his friends drift. As the undertow sweeps, he thinks of Moe (or was it Larry or Curly?), one of the Three Stooges he loved, who yanked a tablecloth and made the dishes leap. My father's near-drowning was like that stunt: the ocean's brutal twirl.

ANOTHER HAUNTING

Our room in Maine faced a quiet inlet. Early one morning, we heard a sound, someone carefully pushing a door open, but both doors were closed. The air stirred. A whirring echoed through the room. That night we had left a small lamp on. In front of it, each time it orbited, the dark shape of a bird.

I MENTION THE DEER

I preferred my friend's father. Mine sat silent in cigar smoke, suave in a cheap suit. Hers, a suburban cowboy, weatherworn in plaid flannel, loud with love. "Aw, girl," he'd say when I visited, patting my cheek. "You're so darn cute." On warm evenings, he'd walk with my friend, head bent to listen, one hand holding their mutt's leash, the other hand around hers.

Around six p.m. each night, I'd listen for his truck, then part the bedroom curtains to watch its slow descent. The truck made happy music—a jangle of rusted lawn mowers and car parts, watering cans and bits of bicycles. My affection for him changed one night, though, when instead of odds and ends, a huge buck, eyes paralyzed in surprise, antlers shocked with blood, filled the truck's bed. I didn't want to believe that he had killed the animal. Or walked to the swing set and unhooked the swings. Or, joined by three neighborhood men who patted him on the back, hung the deer from its hooves like a desecrated god.

HENRIETTA WONDERS WHAT HAUNTS ME

It wasn't his whoop into the deep end, or how his mother had punched out her cigarette, one eye slit in the smoke, before plunging in to save him. And it wasn't their legs churning like chum, or how I inhaled the sky and dove under. No, it was her dress unwrapping in a slow motion striptease, the two sides patterned gills undulating beside her. Her nakedness beneath.

I had never seen a woman undressed, unless the dark teepee under my mother's punishing girdle counts. Then his mother's thrashing legs, and what was between them—horrible, beautiful, red at its heart, pale brown strands like beach glass shimmering.

I TELL HENRIETTA WHY MERMAIDS UPSET ME

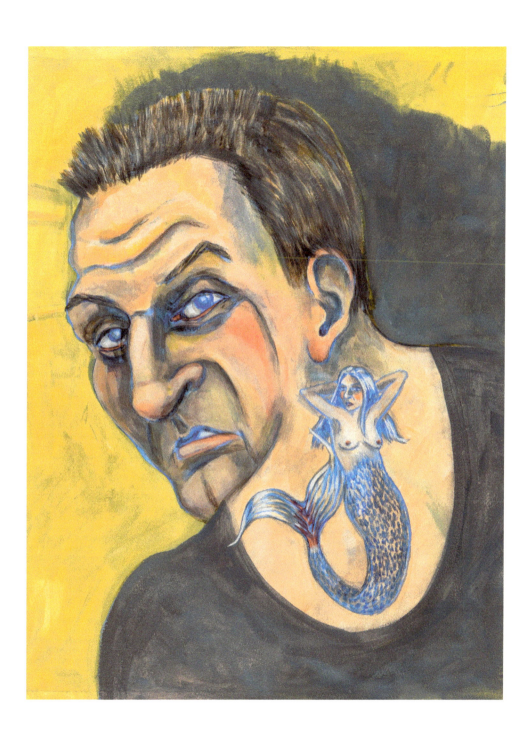

WHY MERMAIDS UPSET ME

After we finish our hot dogs, my mother gives my sister and me a couple of dollars to buy cotton candy. Behind us in line, a man with a tattooed neck—a mermaid, finely drawn and delicately colored—catches me staring.

I expect an indulgent smile, but his bugged-out eyes mock me. His gaze travels from my face to my T-shirt and the flat chest beneath. When he reaches my ankles, he lingers on the lace-trimmed socks. Grimacing, he shakes his head. A small, intentional cruelty.

I MENTION OUR NEIGHBORS' LUAU

Haloed in Marlboro smoke, a few women circled our neighbors' dining table and slivered green tissue paper into grass skirts. A month before that, the hunt for her husband's Hawaiian shirt began. She preferred silk, heavy with hibiscus and purple orchids like the lei she'd wear.

During the luau, their son stayed inside so he couldn't mix with the guests, at least until her husband dragged him out by his pajama collar and flung him into the pool. You could always count on that, and tiki lamps, a red-faced bartender mixing mai tais, and people married to other people kissing in the garage. The next morning, tiny paper parasols of hot pink and bright blue bloomed on the lawn.

THE DEEP END

During his third marriage, my father dressed in creamy sailor suits, owned a boat. Was he afraid of it sinking? I don't know. Talking wasn't his thing. But my sister and I were never scared.

In the shallow end of a Miami pool, a swim coach, burnished and hairy as a coconut, turned our dog paddles into elegant crawls. I felt the caress of his hands, warm even in the cool water, enormous around ours. He'd stare into our eyes as if we were two mermaids imported from New Jersey. "Yes!" he'd say as I flipped on my back, kicking across the long length of blue. When my sister's arms curved into perfect commas, he'd sidestroke to the pool's edge and somersault; an underwater exclamation point.

HENRIETTA HINTS AT SECRETS

One summer I spied a teenage couple, hairless bodies narrow as needlefish. I confess to Henrietta that I had watched them, side by side, bump hips as they strode into lake water tepid as old tea. They stretched their shapes atop the surface, drifted past the moss of curved berm.

Turtles skimmed the surface, heads emitting turtle radar, and then me, hidden in the willows. I parted a drape of frilled green. Two bright spots burned my cheeks as the boy's lips kissed the girl's neck, lowered to her nipple.

THE JITTERING NIGHT

MY FATHER'S MISTRESS

called at two a.m., my mother snoring beside him. The phone rang in their room and on the bedside table between my sister and me, a single siren's scream in the night. Wrenched from sleep, we'd lean in, heads touching, bodies lit. I'd grab the receiver, cover it with my palm. No words, just their breathing; a language we didn't understand. Once, her snort of laughter.

Then months of nothing, until her last call at daybreak. Whether she tried to lure him to love again, or offered a final serenade, I don't know. But after his muffled *'ello*, we heard the clapper of the small bell she shook tinkling.

ED SULLIVAN'S FAULT

I tell Henrietta how the man in a dark suit and dotted bow tie nodded to Ed, then turned to the audience and bowed. The lights lowered. One spot shone white hot on the curtain beside him. The man rotated to his left, raised his arms. With a slant of his hands, a shadow of a wolf leapt into the center of the circle, its ears twitching. The man folded his index finger in and lifted his thumbs, and the wolf became a profile of JFK that grew wings and flew to the perch of his forearm. The audience gasped as a swan drifted from his palms, its neck uncoiling into a regal stalk. Unlike the rabbit-out-of-a-hat trick, I knew the dark images lured from the man's fingers were really magic.

Hand Shadows to Amuse arrived in a brown paper envelope. Every night in my darkened room, I'd take the shade off the lamp and mimic each illustration, twisting my small, clumsy hands into my own "cinema in silhouette": butterfly, camel, elephant, fox.

THE OTHER PLACE?

Henrietta means the apartment where we lived after my parents' divorce. I've described it—one of many brick boxes of four units; ours, second floor left. The rooms smelled thickly of cigarettes and cabbage, and we turned sideways to pass each other in the hall.

Outside, though, old elms and maples made deep swags of shadow and pine trees scrubbed the air. All night, gangs of feral cats stalked the grounds.

Once, when their shrieks woke my mother, she hurled a pot of freezing water out the window. I hated her for that. So did a feline, one eye crusted shut, that flung itself at her, nails first, as she left for work that morning.

BEFORE NANNY CAMS

I told Henrietta that because I had no father, I needed to see how a man and a woman lived together, signs of joined lives. And I wasn't interested in the obvious: shoes left at the door, his-and-her mugs, the commingling of laundry.

When I babysat, I'd slide open medicine cabinets, twist the cap off cologne bottles in faux-wooden cloaks, inhale the limey scent; electric razors moaned when I pressed their switches.

Women's bedside tables were diaries of contradictions: beside a rosary, the flesh-colored orb of a diaphragm, primed for business in its pink plastic case. Beneath a dog-eared copy of *The Scarsdale Diet*, a slice of chocolate-iced yellow cake, wrapped in wax paper.

Most men's drawers held only what they needed: boxes of Trojans, proving sex happened beneath the silky quilted bedspread. Reading glasses for the books they never finished, yellowed receipts never filed.

The most conservative dad, always in a dark boxy suit and unfashionable thick glasses, who offered only a single nod of greeting, surprised me. Eating chocolate chip cookies baked by his wife, at their Formica kitchen table I perused his *Playboy*, collecting crumbs in its centerfold. Then, in the stack of photos I found shoved in the back of his drawer: his two toddler daughters, messy-haired and giggling. His petite wife engulfed in a wedding gown, and between two images of mutts: himself as a child, front tooth missing, gangly body constrained in a stiff Communion suit.

VISITATION

I appreciate a memorable entrance, but a wolf howling and great whooshes of rain are a bit much. Death robbed my father of subtlety. And it was never enough to sense his presence—no whiff of cigar smoke or tinkling piano tunes. No, I had to feel him shifting around in my torso, making a chair of my ribs. Then, looping behind my eyelids, a film of his memories, scratched black and white, all swan necks and shadowed lashes: his girlfriend speaking in a phony Southern accent, *y'all got grits?* Pale legs goose-bumped against a damp gray pier. A nurse, jaunty cap bobby-pinned to a dark bouffant, leaning toward him. "Ed?"

ZEUS, AGAIN

OUTLIERS

In the not-so-swinging '60s suburbs, an artist moved into a basement apartment. He stunk of oil paint and an unfamiliar funk. *Marijuana*, my mother said. Marijuana was something hippies smoked, and I loved all things hippies.

I loved the high school girls promenading past our house in tight knots, daisies sprouting from ponytails. Loved their tough friends too: proud girls in packs; hair teased high, busy with its own personality.

I knew hippies were good, sensed it in my soul. So I wasn't surprised that even after the summer, after no one invited the artist to a softball game, or offered him a charred burger at a barbecue, he showed up with a battered box of oils at the door of a neighborhood girl—awkward, unfriended—and painted an enormous rose on the cast of her broken leg, a petaled planet blooming.

LIFE DRAWING

I tell Henrietta how I walked into the empty studio thirty minutes early and found a model strolling about the room undressed. When they weren't posing, models always wore robes. I set my box of charcoal and pencils down, propped my sketch pad on an easel, and sipped my coffee.

The model seemed so comfortable in his nudity: On the platform he swiveled at the waist, arms raised high above his head in a hairy halo; then lowered himself into an impossible-to-maintain squat. "Would you find this interesting to draw?" he asked, facing me with his arms out in front like a sleepwalker. "Sure," I said, although the pose was lame.

He thanked me, went to a corner of the room where he had stashed a bag, put on his clothes and left. I wondered who the naked man was, but no one else had seen him.

HENRIETTA ASKS ABOUT MY SEX LIFE

The leader of the consciousness-raising group asked the women to describe a sexual fantasy. Seven of us, college seniors, sat blinking into our paper cups of red wine. One member our mothers' age, who tsk-tsked at everything, shrugged and said, "Why the hell not?"

Her fantasy returns in cinematic shorthand: young virgins swim naked in a pool; a god, or some guy in a toga, walks around the perimeter, then points to a blonde and a brunette, who climb out, bow to him, then look at each other in a way that suggests, one: they think he's a schmuck; and two: it's been a long time since they were virgins.

WHAT ABOUT JOY?

Every July 4th, my friends and I stamped a circle in the water of an aboveground pool. Women in bikinis. Men's trunks glowed in shades of bright. One woman wore nothing at all. We sambaed. Cigars like toxic fireflies stunk up the air.

Behind a scraggly grape arbor, the naked woman broke up with her girlfriend. Their parting was good-natured. One found a knife and divided the last slice of vodka-laced watermelon; Naked grabbed a caftan, threw a kiss, and left. We preferred her girlfriend anyway, a jolly librarian with a Mary Poppins accent, who always arrived with books.

OH, THE CARNIES

I tell Henrietta how the flaps of carnival trucks waved like dirty elephants' ears. In a day, the parking lot of our small strip mall reeked of all things sweet, and the twin tracks of the roller coaster carved arches in the sky. Carnies lounged in the sun, smoked in dormant teacups of a ride, snored in its saucers. One's teeth glinted gold. At night they strutted, tough toms, shirts opened to cords of chest hair twisting north of their waistbands, cords I wanted to paddle a boat down. One pulled his girlfriend into the darkness between tents, pushed himself against her. The night jittered with dunk-tank shrieks and mallets whacking moles, but I swear, I could hear her sigh.

ROCK LOBSTER!

In a town with homes named "Blueberry Hill" and two station wagons in every driveway, the Smiths ringed their front door with sloppily painted musical notes and rented their attic to art students. We promised Mrs. Smith that we wouldn't bring boys to bed, which was an easy vow to keep: My boyfriend lived in California and my roommate was gay. Mrs. Smith didn't mind our dinner parties or the reek of my pack-a-day habit. She pretended not to see us drag a potter's wheel up the stairs. But the weekend of the B-52s ended her goodwill—and our lease.

We teased our hair into enormous cones, like gyrating aircrafts, drew wings on our eyes with black liner, invited friends to dance. With the kitchen table jammed against the wall, we pounded the floor. "Rock lobster!" we howled with the chorus. "Rock lobster!" When we didn't hear the phone ringing, Mrs. Smith slammed up the stairs, skidded the needle across the record. "Look," she screamed, pointing to the window. Cop cars sped up to the house, sirens shrieking, the beacons of red lights atop their roofs spinning, spinning.

ZEUS, AGAIN

Something about the guy in the bar bothered me: he grinned too broadly, as if my comments charmed him, leaned in too close as I spoke, was too easy in my company. I said yes, though, when he invited me to a Halloween party. Going through my mother's closet weeks before, I discovered an old caftan in shades of neon rainbow, and welcomed the opportunity to swish around in it.

On the night of the party, I opened the door to discover him dressed as an enormous swan. The costume seemed so lifelike, the eye black, glittering, feathers aflutter. *Whoa!* I said, and tried to back away, but his wings closed around me, one webbed foot wedged in the door.

THE UPSIDE OF LOSS

QUESTIONING THE LAKE

Not language, not the thrill of switching
"dumb with wonder" to "wonder-dumb."
No, what rolls beneath my words
is the first lake I swam in,
the terror of its dark water.

I had only known the burbling aqua
of pools, shallow in their openness,
and then this lapping oval,
its brow of tan stones.

Why did Henrietta's question evoke this lake,
its image lodged now like the shadow of a lover's hand?
Perhaps to cling to pleasure after months of famine,
to feel the lake's fleecy bottom,
how its cool fingers circled my neck
but never let me drown.

UPSIDE OF LOSS

A man wooed me with lavish lilies, early-morning phone calls, silly cards with kittens. After he moved in, he drew a line with a black Sharpie down the center of the refrigerator shelves, dividing his side and mine. If he made the bed, it was only his half, and he wanted to charge me for the Popsicle I took from the freezer. The box had been clearly labeled with his name; I should have known better.

When anonymous notes with words cut from newspapers appeared in my mailbox: *The neighbors named their dog after you* and *Your friends are whores*, I blamed him and kicked him out.

A month later, my garden tomatoes inflated like red beach balls, yellow squash stretched long as ladders, dill grew tall as trees.

VANESSA

I tell Henrietta about a lover, much older than me, with the library of a great scholar—a surprising perk from a man who sold girdles in the Garment District. His room—15-foot ceilings, oak shelves groaning with tomes, a ladder waiting on wheels. In the corner, a desk of mellow mahogany sat grandly on a Persian rug.

I awoke in his bed, desperate to peruse his collection. On entering the room, one book glowed green. When I reached for it, a photo fluttered to the floor. A woman stared. Currents of veins coursed blue as if she were a river contained in spume-pale skin. Ample hips tapered into a whirlpool. What was beneath the water's surface, I didn't know. A glittering fish tail? A shell pearlized pink? Flipping the photo over, a name: "Vanessa." I shook him gently from sleep. *Tell me*, I said.

BEFORE I LEFT MY BOYFRIEND

we had visited a butterfly conservatory. Hot air made our clothes stick. The room hushed. He had been deeply depressed, and the fragility of the insects as they wobbled on his sleeves moved him. Many years later, on the night of his suicide, he stepped from the darkness of a dream to blink in bright light. When I called his name, butterflies spun a blur of ruby.

DOG PSYCHIC

Hannah was depressed after a lover dumped me, her usual sprightly walk slowed to a trudge, her head hanging. Nothing I tried—St. John's wort, a new chew toy—even an organic sirloin—cheered her, so I brought her to a dog psychic and past life regressionist. The psychic nodded, crouched down so she could look into the Lab's eyes. "Come, my poor, sad Hannah," she said, leading the dog to a custom-made love seat, where Hannah reclined.

The psychic placed her fingers on the dog's head and sat silently for a moment. "I can feel the heat of a man's hands as he strokes her belly. And now I see her playing with a puppy. Happy again." She was confident that Hannah would be her old self soon.

It was me the psychic worried about. "May I?" she asked, placing her hands on my head. We sat that way until my scalp tingled. "Oh," she said, blushing. "I can see why you miss him, too."

AND WONDERS ABOUT OLD LOVERS

I used to swim with the mother of an old lover.
We'd pack lunch for the beach, then wade
past the waves until we could no longer feel
the rush of sand and broken shells.

Once, bobbing in easy surf,
we talked about her son,
who no longer wanted me.

"My son is a fool for not loving you," she said,
encircling me in her sea-chilled arms.

It was the closest I had ever felt to anyone.
I kissed her shoulder.

I TELL HENRIETTA ABOUT RUSTY

who wanted to tattoo his name above my navel, like all his other girlfriends. *Rusty*. Life had already drawn on my skin: the silver thread of a cesarean scar, hiked up in one corner. He called it my "second smile." And a more dramatic mark crisscrossed below a hip bone, as if the doctor had sewn with rope instead of thread. But *Rusty*? Fenders rusted after too many snowfalls. Cast-iron skillets, the kind I fried old Rusty's eggs in, rusted. When he ran his hand over my belly and said, "Come on, babe, do it for me," I thought, *Hell no. This guy won't stick around long enough for the ink to dry.*

WHY I MARRIED A SURFER

When my boyfriend and I walked into a bodega, the shop cat, mouse-sated and snoozing, snapped its eyes open and followed us. At the end of the aisle, the cat hurled its heft onto a shelf, where it stood eye-level with my boyfriend. Something passed between them. Some primal recognition I couldn't understand. The cat moved closer, so did he, and they touched noses.

It wasn't the first time that kind of thing had happened. Once, as my love sat reading a book on the cement slab known as my backyard, a glittering of hummingbirds rose from behind the chain-link fence, circled the sky. I was already smitten with his sun-streaked Afro, the puka shell necklace nestled in the dip of his tanned neck, his burritos carnitas. The only creature that had ever visited the backyard was an old crow that looked like the ragged remains of someone's Halloween costume, so the hummingbirds were a sign I couldn't ignore.

HER LIFE NOW

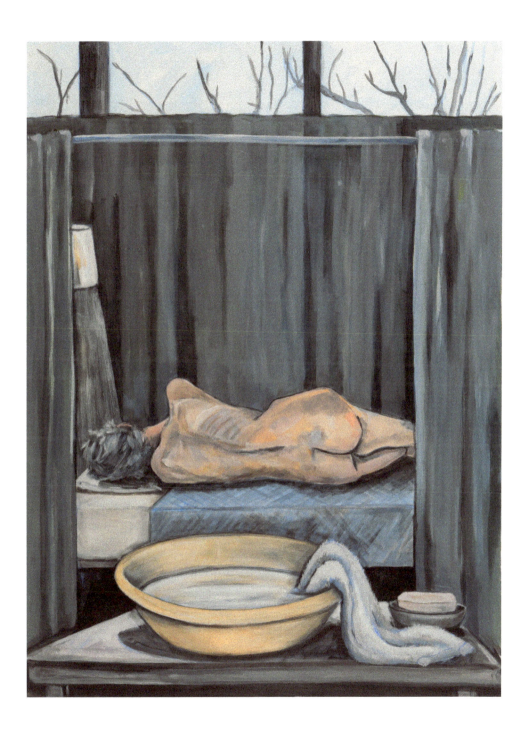

"GHOSTS?" HENRIETTA ASKS

In the room below ours, my mother welcomed visitors to her sleep. A Brownie troop crowded around her bed and stared. Pets dropped in. Old neighbors. One early morning, my husband nudged me awake. "Listen." My mother was laughing, and a minute later, laughed again—a delighted trill, as if she were in the company of someone she adored.

I asked her if she remembered her dream. "Artie was here," she said. Artie. Her lover decades gone. "Um, hmm," I said, but there was no denying her bright cheeks or the hazy cloud of cigar smoke hovering near the bedroom ceiling shaped like Artie's toupee.

WHILE MY MOTHER DREAMS OF JUDGE JUDY

I dream, too. In this dream, Judy's rage ruffles the quiet cutouts of her collar. "Madam!" she shouts at the teen mother whose boyfriend's pit bull bites. First it was the boyfriend and his infected tattoo. Then his five kids. Then the biting dog.

My mother's telling Judy about her girlhood mutt, Shadow, a dark cannonball rolling across the dim light of memory. I see her patent leather shoes, round-toed, pumping as she chases Shadow over hills and onto someone's picnic feast, one paw deep in the center of a chocolate cake, a fried chicken leg clamped in his jaw. "He should have been on a leash!" Judy says. Their laughter pocks lilac trees that open and bloom.

I'm old now; Mother's my child, just like real life. Our home, many homes before, teeters, a teacup on the saucer of the lawn. Her bed, pale blue in the haze, yawns wide. "Buy me a dog," she says, reaching for me in our long-ago kitchen.

HER LIFE NOW

I tell Henrietta how I walked in on an aide bathing my mother in the nursing home. Mother was on her side, turned toward the window. The aide had pulled a rolling table with soap and a big basin of water close by and washed my mother's body, once wide as hawk's wings, now a deflated balloon. Lifting her arm, the aide dipped and wrung, moving the warm cloth over her hands, her hips, between her legs. My mother's voice a near whisper; the aide's too.

When my mother lived with me, I brought soap and warm water to her bedside. "Don't look!" she had screamed.

AFTER,

rivers swirled black, trees pulled from their roots,
tipped to the ground. Falling asleep that evening,
a mouse walked on my pillow and ruffled my hair.
It paused, then scuttled from one side of the bed to another,
as if the bed were a ship alive with strange smells.
I reached for it. Felt tiny sparks of its fear,
its trembling indecision.

My daughter crept into our room when she was little.
She'd lift the blanket, push her body against my side.

I wondered if the mouse had a mother,
and if her nest had washed away.
Then I thought of all mothers,
alert to the night, listening.

HENRIETTA QUESTIONS MY FAITH

HENRIETTA QUESTIONS MY FAITH

Henrietta's face stays patient as some scribbled drawing stashed in my synapses unfolds. Before the images, fragments of voices, suppressed glee. Motel 6, Albuquerque, New Mexico. Five evangelists in bathing suits, waist-deep in the pool. Four men, one woman. God makes a sixth, with a dramatic slant of light. What sins did this woman in her sensible skirted swimsuit commit? It doesn't matter. She's ecstatic, quivering. The pastor's hand rests on her head, another on her shoulder. She clutches her nose, eager for rebirth, oblivious to a rotisserie on the cracked cement near the deep end, each spoke an ellipsis of green chiles, their scent burning in the air.

ARRIVAL

I tell Henrietta how I heard my mother's heartbeat in her womb. I think I'm lying, but as I speak, I feel it in my own chest, the bong*Bong* of it, wavery through the saline sac. My hand, a tiny shimmer of ghost beside my cheek. I hear my mother first, then feel the doctor's wand skidding through the puddle of gel on my belly...no sound, no thud, the terror of that nothingness, until the doctor twists the dial on the machine that brings my daughter's life into the room, her first insistent, pounding, *I'm here*.

IN THE TATTOO SHOP,

I sat before a wall of images: cartoon characters and geisha girls, swans and dragonflies, hearts broken and mended. The artist and I pondered possible designs: a four-leaf clover for a wrist, a goldfish to be hidden in a knee's dimpled flesh. We decided on the word "rose" to be etched beneath a small pink bud on an ankle.

When I laid my infant daughter on the table and held her leg steady, the artist peered down at her trusting face in the bright light, and switched off the inking needle. "I can't," she said. "Please take her and go."

EPILOGUE

THE SWAN RETURNS, THIS TIME WITH A RUSSIAN ACCENT

Before my daughter's wedding, a swan slides
through the dark folds of a lake. Ducks,
feasting on breadcrumbs near the water's lip,
raise their heads and shriek.
Two clouds join and darken. Anyone can see
it's a sign. When the swan glides closer,
I toss a hunk of bread that it snatches,
then sails away like a feathered yacht.

My mother told me a Russian folktale
about a mustached tsarina
infamous for cruelty and terrible gifts.

I've accidentally given some thoughtless presents:
a wedge of cheddar to a lactose-intolerant colleague.
For a boyfriend, a birthday card addressed to my ex.
To a dying relative, a plant that attracted swarms of flies.
I can't beat the tsarina, though, for originality.
She hired artisans to carve a giant swan from ice,
then forced a newly married couple to sleep in it.

A long train trails behind my daughter's white gown.
I'd say she looks like a swan,
but I'm afraid to jinx her.

ABOUT THE PAINTINGS

Artworks

Swan Song, 14" x 11", acrylic/panel, 2023
I Mention the Deer, 22.5" x 15.5", graphite, charcoal, gesso/paper, 2023
Why Mermaids Upset Me, 21" x 17", acrylic/paper, 2023
Night Memory, 15" x 13", pencil, acrylic/paper, 2021
Night Angel, 10.5" x 9", acrylic/paper, 2021
And Wonders about Old Lovers, 14" x 10", graphite, acrylic/paper, 2023
My Mother's Life, 30" x 22", acrylic/paper, 2023
Henrietta Questions My Faith, 30" x 22", charcoal/paper, 2023
Rest, 14" x 11", pencil, acrylic/paper, 2021

Collaborator's Statement

Our first collaboration, *I Tell Henrietta*, came about organically. We're longtime friends and storytellers who narrate with different mediums and admire each other's work. We tend to share a similar aesthetic: mercurial with glints of humor. The poems and illustrations with the same titles were direct collaborations: I would share several pages of poetry with Kristin, who chose those that resonated with her, and she turned my words into visual characters that live in full color on the page. Then, I visited her studio and selected the remaining art. The swan, a recurring image in the book, swam out of the water and onto a character's head. We couldn't resist using the painting for the cover.

—Tina Barry, author

ACKNOWLEDGMENTS

Gratitude to Lissa Kiernan for Henrietta and for giving *I Tell Henrietta* a home. Henrietta for keeping me afloat when the lake engulfed me. Kristin Flynn, friend and collaborator. The members of my writers' groups, thank you for your good counsel, and for the laughs. Proofreader: Cindy Hochman of "100 Proof" Copyediting Services for her eagle eyes. My mother, Rosalind Ehlin, dearest one. My friends Deirdre Sinnott, Cathy Arra, and Jane Siegel Strumpf—I'm lucky to have you in my life. Claudia Mallea, brilliant survivor. And to my sister, Tamara Ehlin, the bravest person I know.

Thank you to the publishers, editors, and readers of the journals and anthologies in which the following poems first appeared, sometimes in different forms:

Agape Editions: "I Tell Henrietta about Rusty"
A-Minor: "After," (Wigleaf Top 50 2024 longlist)
Bending Genres: "And Wonders about Old Lovers," "Henrietta Wonders What Haunts Me," "Henrietta Questions My Faith"
Five Minutes: "Life Drawing"
Flash Frontier's *A Cluster of Lights* anthology: "Dog Psychic"
Ghost City Review: "Another Haunting"
Gone Lawn: "'Ghosts?' Henrietta Asks," "Henrietta Asks about My Sex Life," "So, Your Father"
MacQueen's Quinterly: "Telling Lies" (nominated for Best Microfiction); "Outliers," "Ed Sullivan's Fault"
Maryland Literary Review: "I Mention the Deer," "My Year of Drawing Swans"
Nixes Mate: "I Tell Henrietta about Judge Judy," "My Father's Mistress"

South Florida Poetry Review: "Why Mermaids Upset Me," "In the Tattoo Shop," "The Swan Returns, This Time with a Russian Accent," "Upside of Loss," "Zeus, Again," "Vanessa," "Visitation"

The Mackinaw: a journal of prose poetry: "Before Nanny Cams," "I Mention the Deer"

Thimble Literary Magazine: "Her Life Now," "Arrival," "Why Chinchilla Is My Favorite Fur," "The Other Place?"

trampset: "Oh, the Carnies" (Nominated for the Best of the Net Award)

Unbroken: "Questioning the Lake," "A New Kind of Drowning," "Henrietta Hints at Secrets," "Why I Married a Surfer"

Yellow Mama Literary Magazine: "I Tell Henrietta about Judge Judy"

ABOUT THE AUTHOR

I Tell Henrietta is Tina Barry's third full-length collection. Tina has been published widely in newspapers, magazines, literary journals, and anthologies, including *Rattle*, *Verse Daily*, and *The Best Small Fictions 2020* (spotlighted story) and 2016.

Tina holds an MFA in creative writing from Long Island University, Brooklyn. She's been nominated several times for the Pushcart Prize, Best of the Net, and Best Microfiction awards. Tina is a teaching artist at the Poetry Barn and Writers.com. She lives in New York's Hudson Valley with her husband, the ceramic artist Bob Barry.

ABOUT THE ARTIST

Kristin Flynn earned a BFA in fashion design from Parsons School of Design, an AAS degree in Textiles from Rochester Institute of Technology, and studied painting at Marylhurst University in Portland, Oregon. Her paintings and drawings have been exhibited in numerous group and solo shows, including the Cheryl McGinnis Gallery, Stone Ridge Center for the Arts, Jane Street Gallery, Studio 89, Brick Gallery, Kingston Museum of Contemporary Art, and Bard College.

Kristin's residencies include the Vermont Studio Center in Johnson Vermont, Jentel Foundation in Sheridan, Wyoming, and the Platte Clove A.I.R. in Arkville, New York. Kristin had an extensive career in the fashion industry as an apparel designer at Nike in Portland, Oregon. She created and directed a fashion design degree program at SUNY Ulster Community College.

ABOUT THE PUBLISHER

AIM Higher publishes books that blur boundaries, negate binaries, interrogate, confound, and delight. We endeavor to open portals into unmapped and magical dimensions, and hold deep respect for intuition and collaboration.

Also from Aim Higher

Lissa Kiernan *The Whispering Wall*
Kim Noriega *Naming the Roses*

COLOPHON

I Tell Henrietta is set in Anivers and Freight Text Pro. The Dutch artist Jos Buivenga created the elegant yet whimsical Anivers to commemorate *Smashing Magazine*'s first anniversary. Joshua Darden's Freight Collection draws inspiration from the warmth and practicality of 18th-century Dutch typefaces.

Printed in the USA
CPSIA information can be obtained
at www.ICGtesting.com
LVHW012342171024
794118LV00026B/100